A RENAISSANCE MAN

PETER M. KATSAROS

BERWICK COURT PUBLISHING CO.

Chicago, IL

Peter M. Katsaros is a nationally-known trial lawyer, law professor, public speaking consultant and man of letters.

He writes on occasion with the pen name Voltaire.

The characters in the fiction section of the book are the author's invention and have no relationship to real people, living or dead.

Berwick Court Publishing Company

Chicago, Illinois

http://www.berwickcourt.com

Contents

Dedicated To ...

Joanne for a marriage of exceptional beauty and zest and fun;

Beth, for a marriage heaven sent and for the gifts of our Hollywood-handsome, talented children;

Sarah, Steve and Molly;

Matt and Stacey, Patrick, Charley and Jackson;

Kathryn and Burke;

Chris and Emily and the community of saints who have loved my family so well all these years.

You know who you are.

My buoyancy I owe to you.

Ɦeroic Ԝriters

I must Create a System or be enslav'd by another Man's
I will not Reason or Compare: my business is to Create

> -William Blake, British poet, artist and
> saint in his *Poet's Motto*

The greatest tie of all is language … Words are the only
things that last forever….

> -Winston S. Churchill, excerpted from
> "The Union of the English Speaking
> Peoples," May 15, 1938

We shall not flag or fail. We shall go on to the end. We shall
fight despair in France, we shall fight despair on the seas and
oceans, we shall fight with growing confidence every day,
we shall defend our family against despair, whatever the cost
may be, we shall fight it on the beaches, in the fields and

the streets, we shall never surrender to despair, nor will we allow anyone in our family to do so. We devote ourselves to leading the family into broad, sunlit uplands.

-A pledge to my family adapted from the remarks of Winston S. Churchill on June 4 and 18, 1940. I made this pledge in January 2001 and have repeated it hundreds of times since.

Introduction

THE DONUT HAS A SPECIAL place in my heart and, I would bet, also in the hearts and minds of native Chicagoans—Boomers through Millenials. For most of us born and raised in the land of politically active dead Democratic voters, the donut brings to mind a Chicago city worker on coffee break, or on the clock but sitting in a city truck in the shade of a tree. Or, equally as likely, a Chicago cop on duty, dozing in a squad car with coffee and donut crumbs sprinkled over an ample belly reined in by a strained and nowhere-to-be-seen belt.

The lead story in this collection mainly introduces real Chicagoans. Judge Donut, shows that a love for donuts, the easy way out and the need to cheat to win affects some lawyers and judges, like some city workers. And that bend in the ethical road toward crime confronts both workers in law and public life every day. Handling power responsibly and ethically is difficult for many.

Heed this warning. Just like the steadfast prophet Jeremiah told his people, sometimes unsuccessfully, "listen up." Find out who the Judge Donuts really are and stay out of their courtrooms in the Cook County Circuit Court's Daley Center if you are looking for a fair trial. Or, if you happen to be an investigative journalist looking for an exciting story and a way to keep your high-risk career alive a few weeks longer, go get this guy. The Pulitzer is a cinch. Do not give up. Woodward and Bernstein were hungry young journalists once. Just ask Jack Warden, who played their most sympathetic metropolitan news editor. I heard him say so in the film *All The President's Men*.

To all this talk of donuts, my wife responds, "Sounds good, but don't donuts appeal to many people—chubby, slim or in between? And, aren't donuts and the coffee that comes with them within reach of many Chicagoans from all walks of life?" I savor Joanne's ideas as much as her figure. She is right, as usual.

My earliest memory of donuts came from my ninth year and the Sunday trips to Millie's, a corner deli in the Little Flower neighborhood on Chicago's south side, in which my big Greek family thrived for thirteen laughter-drenched years. There, I found the best gourmet cake donuts I have ever tasted. The chocolate donuts were fresh cake and slathered with curls upon mounting curls of rich chocolate frosting. One of these made a kid's Sunday heavenly, hours before the tasty communion and pungent incense grabbed our senses back. Two of those sweet beauties inspired an essay like this five decades later. But, if you were really clever and shrewd, two donuts might give you the stomach ache upon which you could mount a plea to be excused from Sunday school and the rather somber three-hour Greek Orthodox Sunday service. I never tried that, but my younger brother used the strategy over and over again with astounding success.

I have written the following stories, essays, poems and letters mostly about Chicagoans in the 21st century. These Chicagoans are fortunate to live in what has become in the last twenty years the Paris of America. Our flowers, public parks and public landscaping, architecture, sculpture, theatres and cultural life, promenades and the jeweled eighteen-mile kiss of Lake Michigan lakefront puts this sparkling metropolis of seven million plus in the top rank of the world's beauties. Despite Chicago's dazzling place on the world map of aesthetic and artistic cities, Judge Donut reminds us, this town is still a city on the make and occasionally, a city on the take.

But, we can all take comfort in our many traditions, our coffee and donuts and the fact that our stellar United States Attorney's office works 24/7.

Stories

Judge Donut

JUDGE EVAN LAFAYETTE DANAUET WADDLED
into his courtroom, 4108, in the Daley Center in Chicago
at 10:23 a.m. with a hangover. Like a hockey player he rocked
from side to side. Both of his hips hurt with every step. A
sickening three hundred and sixty-nine pounds on a five-foot-
five-inch frame, the judge had been out drinking at Gibson's
until 3:30 a.m. with a hottie, Carol Lombard. Things had
been going well, especially well after Carol's fourth dirty mar-
tini. She had been touching him in all the right places. The
layers of flesh in which his manliness had been entombed had

given way to her deft strokes. Emboldened by the six Manhattans that he had downed and with his confidence rising, he invited her back to his condo in Old Town for the blessed event. Carol kissed him on the cheek, screwed up her face at his sour smell and promptly left the joint. As painful as it was to watch her gorgeous rump bounce and weave on her exit, Evan did his manly duty. Next time for sure.

The judge was pissed. Just spent $400 for an erection. His vision of Carol's curves and points undulating into an ecstatic frenzy dashed on the wrong rocks, the Honorable Evan inhaled two more Maker's Mark "perfect" Manhattans. He then stumbled down north Dearborn Street to slide into bed next to his lover of last resort, Wallace Geor, the Cardinal of the Roman Catholic Archdiocese of Chicago.

Judge Danauet passed gas as he entered his private chambers, quickly closing the door behind him to avoid any embarrassment with his clerk, Deborah Chambers. He slowly slid into his high back leather chair resting his aching head and looking upward into a wall of two hundred books. Not law books, mind you, not law treatises, not case reports—two hundred hardback detective novels. At $20-30 a pop, the clean unblemished book jackets of $6000 worth of novels faced the nauseated jurist.

Danauet loved fantasy and escape far more than he loved justice. In fact, he cared not a whit for justice—whatever that was. What got Evan up in the morning was his thirst for erotic highs and power. Only those two insatiable needs dominated his waking hours. Male lovers, female lovers – it did not matter. He was in the hunt for imaginative lovers with zest in their moves, and for more and more power and status as a judge. And the older and heftier he got and the more of a sloth he became, the daily hunt to satisfy his lusts became more difficult. Loser, he thought of himself too often these days.

A knock at the door hurt the judge's head. Was he bleeding on his brain? Everything hurt the judge's head, even breathing. Before he could respond, Deborah Chambers, the court clerk, stuck her head into the chambers. "Judge, we just heard from the Chief Judge. A case for trial has just been assigned to you: Timmons v. Bowerman Dairy."

"Goddamn time that nigger did something for me. What's it about?"

"Race discrimination—black truck driver claims he was pushed to the back of the bus when he tried to get promoted and then canned when he bitched."

"Ah, the race card … I bet the nigger is using the case to shake down the company for money for crack or broads. Deb, get me the trial briefs. Then, call the lead counsel for both sides and tell them to be here at two in the afternoon to talk about the case. And, tell them that if they are a minute late, I will fine them $1,000."

"Yes, Judge."

The door to the judge's chambers closed once again allowing the suffering jurist to nestle into his leather chair for a brief nap before the trial briefs arrived. The judge dozed, reminiscing about trysts with call girls and a few young nuns.

Harry Petrakis left the courthouse after receiving the assignment of the Timmons case to Judge Danauet and walked slowly toward his law office at Adams and Wells in downtown Chicago. He was understandably worried—Danauet, a racist hack on the bench; a creep defense counsel; a well-paid defense team—the usual disadvantages a union labor lawyer faced every day.

Harry Pericles Petrakis was fifty years old. "Named after Harry Mark Petrakis, Chicago's most distinguished Greek man of letters, Harry Petrakis the union labor lawyer had just reached a hard fought for dream: a named partnership and a large equity stake in Chicago's most successful union labor law firm. It had been a long time coming with Winston Churchill-sized hurdles along the way. Twenty-two lawyers strong with several of Chicago's finest labor unions as the anchor clients, Petrakis' firm was a major player in labor circles. Harry was the firm's trial lawyer.

Harry crossed Madison Street and ducked into the vestibule of a Greek Orthodox Church. He hastily lit four candles in honor of his mother and father and his grandparents before entering this sacred space.

Sitting in the pew at the back, Harry crossed himself three times and started to calm down. He looked up at the polished gold on the altar, the gold surrounding the somber-faced, haloed saints in their five-foot icons. Harry loved this church and the warmth of the Greek family and community that had loved him so well. The Greek Orthodox churches of Chicago held spectacular religious rituals where joy and solemnity were in exquisite balance.

Harry said a prayer, "Do justice, love kindness, walk humbly with God," a one-liner from Micah. He crossed himself again and walked the two blocks south to his firm.

Upon entering the reception area of the firm, he greeted Ray Timmons with a smile and a handshake, offered him a Coke and walked him into the large conference room. The huge mahogany conference table was surrounded by twenty finely crafted French provincial chairs. Timmons sat in one of them and asked timidly, "Mr. Petrakis, what do you think of the judge?"

"I am worried about him; Ray. Danauet is a hack. Tomorrow we pick a jury and start with you. I expect the defense to try and knock as many blacks and Hispanics and union people off the jury as the judge will allow."

Petrakis then worked with his client getting him ready for his direct and cross-examination. Timmons left about seven in the evening. Petrakis finished his sixteenth hour of work at eight and then hopped a cab home.

The battle was on. Petrakis was thrilled.

Micah Hirsh, the defense attorney, also walked south after the case assignment to Danauet. He wound his way down LaSalle to a gritty area south of the el. In a dingy, unwashed armpit of the Loop, his firm sat across from an adult book store. Hirsh loved the place but once got caught by his wife, his firm manager, exiting it. There was hell to pay. Lysistrata was a bitch, then and now.

Hirsh was the son of a respected rabbi whose loving ways skipped a generation. Micah was a bully. He lied as naturally as he breathed, only faster. His mood swings were frequent.

Micah raged at his staff and opponents when things did not go his way. Shouting matches with his wife Sarah were a daily event. Only one lawyer ever worked for Hirsh for more than a year. That was his current associate, a lanky lawyer named Rafa Khan—"Rock" to his Domer fraternity brothers. Like Hirsh, Khan misrepresented the facts and the law often in state courtrooms. He was more careful in federal court but not much. Khan despised Hirsh and was vocal about it to those within earshot.

Micah stormed into his office. "Sarah, where is that bitch, Ryan? Get her ass in here. I have a Hawks game."

Sarah shook her head and called Carol Catherine Ryan, the President of Bowerman Dairy Company, the defendant. Carol was walking down the steps of Holy Name Cathedral, answering her cellphone. "Hello, Sarah, running late, just got out of Mass. The Cardinal gave this rambling homily on celibacy. Such bullshit. Thinking of becoming Episcopalian. I am grabbing a cab. So sorry."

"Carol, be careful around Micah. He is on a rampage."

"Sarah, I am the client, remember? Micah should worry about my moods. Fuck him." Carol crossed herself. She regretted it but swearing made her feel better.

Minutes later Carol sat in Micah's office amid six disheveled banker's boxes. "Micah, this place is a mess. Did you take care of the judge? How long will this take? I have a business to run."

"I paid the judge in cash from the money you paid on the last bill for trial preparation. I drew the money out of my operating account so it cannot be traced back to you. I don't know how the judge plans to deliver justice."

"Fuck justice. I am not here for philosophy. I paid to win. I am not paying that nigger and slime ball Greek bastard of his $300,000. I will sue you for malpractice if this does not work. You are not the only fixer in town, just the cheapest."

"Carol, tomorrow we pick the jury. We keep blacks, union members and liberals off the jury. Not worried about Hispanics in most cases, especially the working class ones. There are plenty of black/ Hispanic tensions in Chicago that may work to our advantage. We will have three peremptory challenges and an unlimited number of "cause" challenges to use in knocking off people we do not like."

"Danauet better take care of it or your insurer will be paying."

"I will meet you in Courtroom 4108 tomorrow at 8:45 a.m."

"Fine. Get this over with."

Carol Ryan cabbed over to The University Club of Chicago on Michigan Avenue to pick up her Jaguar for the drive home to Winnetka, to her tony suburb home. Micah Hirsh cabbed to the Hawks game where he met Rafa Khan, for trial prep: boozing and screaming.

Judge Danauet kept everyone waiting the first day of trial. Everyone in the case was to be ready by 8:45 a.m. The prospective jurors had been brought up to 4108 by 9:00 a.m. and deposited into benches in the courtroom. The judge took the bench at 9:20 a.m. He kept everyone standing for several minutes as he took the bench. He stood erect and surveyed the courtroom. He felt good and boomed: "You may be seated."

"Good morning. I am Judge Danauet. You are here to be interviewed for jury service in Timmons v. Bowerman Dairy Company, an employment discrimination case. Representing the plaintiff Ray Timmons is Harry Petrakis, sitting on my left. Representing the defendant Bowerman Dairy is Micah Hirsh, a fine lawyer. Mr. Hirsh and his client, Carol Ryan, the president of the company, are on my right."

"I will ask you questions to help the lawyers and me decide if you can fairly decide this case. The lawyers may question you. Then, we will choose the jury. Pay strict attention.

9

If I find anyone asleep, I will hold you in contempt." The prospective jurors looked down. A young Millennial giggled. Danauet did not notice given his enthrallment with his command and the opening solemnities.

Four jurors were chosen without controversy—three Caucasian women and a middle-aged Hispanic woman who lived in a largely black West Side neighborhood near Madison and Keeler. Hirsh thought that this juror would have a better than 50% chance of disliking blacks like Timmons.

The inquiry then turned to a young black man named Reggie Black. Black mumbled his answers to the judge's questions and looked rather menacing when he was not looking down and away from the judge. When Micah Hirsh started, Black startled everyone by asking Hirsh if he was "a murder lawyer." Hirsh, looking annoyed, said no. Black quickly followed with: "How much you make?" At that point the judge intervened telling Black that the question was inappropriate. Twittering of the old fashioned kind began in the jury box.

Hirsh decided to use a peremptory challenge against Reggie Black, the first challenge used during the process. Petrakis let the challenge pass without comment, viewing Black as hostile. He kept his powder dry for the first hint of discrimination by Hirsh. The judge excused Black from jury duty.

The next prospect was a forty-seven-year-old Hispanic woman, Elena Santos. Petrakis liked her instantly. She smiled in a friendly warm way. She was an elementary school teacher in Forest Park, just west of Chicago. Hirsh worried about her. Too well educated, too open minded, and a possible foreperson. Zeroing in on her personal life, Hirsh found out that she had five children and had never been married. He pounced in a conference off to the side of the bench with the judge and Petrakis.

"Judge, I am going to use a peremptory challenge against

Miss Santos." He looked pleased.

"Mr. Petrakis?"

"Judge, I am making a Batson challenge. This woman is an educator with a good work history. She is being challenged because she is a racial minority."

"Mr. Hirsh?" Danauet was bored and barely listened to the lawyer debate. He wondered how much Petrakis' taupe Brooks Brothers suit cost and whether he was gay. Hirsh broke the daydream with his aggravating voice.

"Judge, she is unmarried with five children!" Hirsh was outraged at five children out of wedlock. He looked at the judge expecting Danauet to chime in with a heavy dose of contempt.

Petrakis responded, "Judge, the defendant has shown its discriminatory intent. Santos is supporting these children. She is a thoughtful professional woman and will make a good juror. I ask you to sustain the challenge. That unmarried woman stuff is a pretext for discrimination."

Danauet flexed his cgo. "Mr. Petrakis, I overrule your objection and allow the challenge. MISSS Santos will be excused. She can return to teaching and raising her litter. Though Mr. Hirsh's explanation for his objection is incredibly offensive, it is not a federal constitutional violation.

Hirsh was thrilled in getting a jury with no blacks, one Hispanic, eleven Caucasians and no one with any empathic leanings. Six men and six women. Petrakis' instincts told him he was in trouble with Judge Donut but he held out hope for the jury.

The trial started with opening statements. Petrakis'

beautifully crafted opening was blown apart landmine-fashion twelve times by inappropriate objections by Hirsh. Most objections were sustained. Danauet prevented Petrakis from using his best exhibits in the opening statement because of spurious objections by Hirsh. The judicial muscle spent ruling on the many heated objections created a tense and hostile climate for Petrakis and his client, giving the jurors the false impression that Timmons' lawyer was acting improperly. Unethical as it was, Hirsh was having great fun busting up the flow of Petrakis' critically important presentation. Danauet dozed dreaming of Carol Lombard's breasts.

Hirsh let Kahn give the defense opening. Khan had never done a jury trial and was terrified. He started telling the jurors that his client Carol Ryan had been a popular beer taster at the brewery near her college. Petrakis laughed hysterically inside his head at the ineptitude.

Khan made a pathetic attempt to get the jury to like his well-heeled client by humanizing her. Not easy to do given Ryan's perch in wealthy Winnetka, from her membership in the North Shore parish fondly called "Faith, Hope and Cadillacs" to the haughty attitude that she would soon show as a witness. Petrakis made several objections during the defense opening to facts that the defense would never be able to prove. All were overruled. Each time Danauet made the ruling he stood up in his chair and publicly castigated Petrakis. The fix was in, it appeared. Petrakis stayed calm pondering a Buddhist teaching: "Life is difficult."

Khan finished his rambling, sophomoric opening. He sat down drained. The judge smiled at him and thanked him.

Danauet barked at Petrakis: "Mr. Petraaakissss, call your first witness if you have any."

"Your honor, we call the Plaintiff, Ray Timmons."

Ray Timmons walked to the witness stand, was sworn

in and looked at the jury finding no peers. He then looked at his lawyer.

Timmons testified on direct examination for about an hour and a half telling the jury how he had capably handled the dairy truck job in several suburbs south of Chicago.

Petrakis asked about Timmons' hiring.

"I was hired on the spot by my boss, Finnian Tice. He told me he liked my experience and he was short-handed because a number of his union dairy drivers were taking their summer vacations."

Petrakis queried: "Ray, how long did it take you on this new job before you got a regular delivery route and handled it by yourself?"

"Two days, sir."

Petrakis paused for emphasis turning toward the jurors. He moved to underscore the point: "Only two days?"

"Just two days. I had two years workin' as a beverage driver in Lincoln Park before I took this job with the dairy. Took me two days to learn the route through four suburbs way south."

"What suburbs? What route?"

"They gave me far south suburbs—Markham, Harvey, Country Club Hills, Lansing. They told me I could carry a gun as long as it was registered." Hirsh and Khan giggled at that answer.

"Why would you need a gun?"

"Other drivers been robbed—one of them shot and killed. On some deliveries you get paid with checks or cash."

"On the average, how much money would you collect on that route daily?"

"Averaged $9,000 a day. Highest day was $15,000."

"Ray, did you like this driving job?"

"Yes, a lot. Good hours—started by 6:30 a.m., done

by 3:30 in the afternoon. Job kept me in good shape, lifting crates of milk and walking eight hours a day. Didn't need to work out."

Timmons looked the part he played in this drama. Standing 5'11" he was a strong, buff former high school fullback who took pains to stay in shape. He was a deadly serious man with little formal education who had grown up in foster homes all over the poorest parts of Chicago and Waukegan.

Timmons wore a clean, ill-fitting blue shirt and plain black slacks the first day of trial. His lawyer had asked him to wear a sport coat only to be told that he did not own one, nor a suit.

"Ray, what were you paid for this work?"

"I was paid hourly. Came out to about $35,000 a year. No benefits – no vacation, no sick days, no insurance, a few holidays."

"Ray, were there better jobs at Bowerman Dairy than the one you started on?"

"Yes, the best job—the one I was after—was the union truck-driving job. Paid $50,000 to $60,000 salary a year, came with health insurance, sick days, pension plan and vacation under the Teamsters contract."

"Did you go after that job?"

"Sure did—starting the day I was hired. I know all about union driving jobs."

"What do you mean?"

"Mr. Tice told me when he hired me that I would be the next union driver hired into a full-time position, if I showed him I could do the work."

"When did you talk to Mr. Tice about the union job next after you started working for the dairy?"

"'Bout three months after I started a union driver job opened up when one of the older drivers retired. I heard about

14

it and asked Mr. Tice if I could have the job."

"And?"

"He said no. The job was going to Ryan Tice."

"Who was Ryan Tice? He was a skinny white kid 'bout nineteen years old with some connection to the owners of the dairy company. Weighed about 125 pounds and was so weak he needed help to load his truck. Had to drive his route with a helper to help unload the crates."

"Were you upset with Finnian Tice, your boss?"

"Sure, I told him he had promised me the next open union driver job."

"What did he say when you brought that up?"

"He said: 'next time Ray. That's all I can say. Don't like it, get out. Plenty of guys waiting to take your place.'"

The jurors followed Timmons testimony closely. Petrakis knew how to deliver absorbing storytelling with vivid detail. Hirsh and his sidekick, Danauet, were restless.

The story got better.

"How many other union driving jobs opened up after that?"

"Three more, sir. Every two months one opened up as the older white drivers were retiring or went off on disability when their backs gave out."

"Did you visit Mr. Tice and apply for each one?"

"Yes, the day I heard of each opening."

"Did you ever get promoted to that union driving job you were promised?"

"No. The second job went to Paul Sinarski. The third to his cousin George Sinarski and the fourth to James Pucinski. All of them had less experience than me. All three of them were born in Europe, Poland, I think."

"What happened when you found you could not get promoted?"

"First, I went to talk to the Teamsters union steward. He would not get involved. He told me to shut up and get back to work. Then, after Pucinski got hired I talked to a friend of mine at the Alderman's office in Englewood where I lived. She told me to file a charge of race discrimination with the U.S. Equal Employment Opportunity Commission."

"Did you?"

"I did, the day I got fired by Mr. Tice."

"Explain that please."

"After work I went to see Mr. Tice and told him that he was discriminating against me and I was going to the EEOC about it."

"What did he say?"

"He got mad, told me that they could not have any lawsuits around here and told me that we were done. I asked him if he was firing me and he said 'yes.' I got my stuff from my locker and went to the EEOC that day to file a charge of race discrimination."

"Did the EEOC investigate the charge?"

"Yes, it took them over a year to do their work but they came back and found that I had been discriminated against because I was black. But, the dairy would not take me back or give me the union job, so I filed this suit."

"Thank you Ray. Your Honor, I pass the witness."

Judge Danauet motioned toward the defense table. Hirsh moved toward the podium with some notes in his trembling hands. He wore a rumpled Joseph A. Bank suit. It had not been cleaned in months. A grey and blue checked tie on a dark blue shirt filled out the attire. Hirsh had lifted the tie from a friend's funeral parlor. They had been chatting during an embalming session. When Hirsh's friend hurried off to meet a new customer Micah helped himself. What are friends for?

16

The cross-examination began. "Mr. Timmons, do you have a felony conviction?"

Ray Timmons looked down, admitting that he had one for an altercation with some Chicago policemen three years earlier. He then admitted that he had been sentenced to two years of probation. He never had any trouble since.

"That is all we need to know, Mr. Timmons. Judge, we are done with this guy."

"I understand Mr. Hirsh." A smile lit up Judge Danauet's visage.

"Mr. Petrakis, what else do you have before the plaintiff rests his case?"

"Judge, I would like to introduce a set of business records showing the daily route assignments of the dairy drivers, attendance and tardiness for the year that Mr. Timmons worked for the defendant."

"Mr. Hirsh, any objection to the admission of this group exhibit."

"Yes, Judge, the exhibit is irrelevant, self-serving and prejudicial."

Danauet was irritated by Hirsh's unfamiliarity with the Illinois Rules of Evidence. Brushing aside Hirsh's ignorance, the judge disposed of the nonsense quickly. "The document is admitted and the objection overruled. Mr. Hirsh, there is no evidence objection entitled self-serving or prejudicial. Don't waste our time with objections like that again."

Hirsh whispered a profane remark to Carol Ryan and Rafa Khan.

Danauet glared at the plaintiff's trial table and roared, "Mr. Petrakis, what else do you have? This case, if you call it that, has gone on far too long."

Harry jumped to his feet saying: "Our last witness, your Honor, is Frank Martinez."

Frank Martinez, a husky fifty-four-year-old warehouse-man, was sworn in and took the witness stand looking scared.

Petrakis began the direct examination establishing that Martinez was a twenty-year employee of Bowerman Dairy who helped the drivers load their trucks in the morning and unload them at night. During the day he unloaded trucks delivering fresh dairy products into refrigerated storage.

Then, Petrakis went for the gold.

"Mr. Martinez, do you know a union driver named George Sinarski?"

"Yes sir, I do."

"How long have you known him?"

"About three or four years as long as he has been with the dairy company."

"Did you ever hear Mr. Sinarski make racial remarks while at work?"

"Yes, sir. Many times, just about every day he worked."

"What did you hear him say?"

"I heard him say, 'Heil Hitler' every other day and then he would yell in the warehouse that 'we should just round up the niggers, spics and Jews and kill them all.'"

"Now, when Sinarski made these loud remarks was Ray Timmons ever there?"

"Yes, sir, I remember Ray being there. Sinarski always made those remarks when Ray and one or both of the two other black drivers were near him."

"Do you know if Finnian Tice was ever in the warehouse when Sinarski went off on blacks, Hispanics and Jews?"

Nervously, Martinez paused a while and then quietly said, "I think so."

Harry Petrakis, displaying the best poker face in town, was leaping for joy at this direct evidence of discrimination in the workplace. For some reason that only God and the saints know, Martinez had told the truth to the government investigator probing Timmons' charge of discrimination for the EEOC. Petrakis got a copy of the government's interview of Martinez that disclosed these racist remarks. Harry made sure that Martinez knew he had it in the months before the trial.

Micah Hirsh put on his best unfazed look at the defense table, rising to dismiss the Martinez testimony with: "Judge we see no reason to cross-examine."

Then, Petrakis spoke confidently, looking directly at Danauet: "Judge, the Plaintiff rests his case."

Judge Danauet abruptly stood up, thus compelling everyone in the courtroom to rise just as quickly, except for the juror in the back row that had fallen asleep. Danauet hit the roof upon noticing the juror with his hands politely folded over his sixty-inch waist. The Judge's Deputy Sherriff bailiff was ordered to go over and shake the weary juror back into public duty. When the juror woke and stood next to his peers, Danauet told him that another sleeping episode would be a contempt of court and earn a night in the infamous Cook County Jail. For the remainder of the trial this chagrined juror sipped a can of Red Bull at every break.

"Members of the jury, the Plaintiff, Ray Timmons, has rested his case and now you will hear the evidence offered by the Defendant, Bowerman Dairy Company. Mr. Hirsh, call your first witness."

"Thank you Judge. We call Mr. Finnian Tice."

A tiny man no more than 140 pounds dripping wet wearing faded brown slacks, a blue button-down shirt and a sloppily knotted green tie sat in the witness chair. His reddish hair was thinning.

"Please tell the jury your full name and the town in which you live." Hirsh had never tried a jury case before this one. But, he had always been thrilled by the sound of his own voice. His father's dream that he would become a cantor died a long time ago.

"My name is Finnian Aloysius Tice. People at work call me Finn. I live in the Beverly neighborhood of Chicago and I go to church."

"What church?"

Harry Petrakis knew that this evidence was irrelevant but could not risk objecting to it for fear of offending any religious jurors.

"I go to Christ the King Roman Catholic Church and every once in a while I drive into the Loop to Old St. Patrick's Church. I am studying to be a deacon in the church."

Petrakis was beside himself. One more question about Tice's religion and he was going to ask for a sidebar conference with the judge to object to the religion emphasis. Hirsh moved on to something else. He loved cheating and escaping without a scratch. He fancied himself the Jewish Joseph Kennedy Sr.

"Finn, what is your job with the dairy and how long have you worked there?"

"I manage the drivers and the warehousemen for the company—about forty employees." An Irish brogue was still present in his voice, twenty years after his emigration.

"Were you always the manager at the dairy?" Hirsh wondered how the judge was going to steer the case toward a not guilty for the Dairy. Danauet had not been very encouraging of the defense lately.

"No sir, for six maybe seven years I worked as a union driver. Only got the manager's job when the prior manager was killed in a bar fight after a Bears game."

"Finn, do you know the plaintiff, Ray Timmons?"

"Yes, sir, he was one of the temporary drivers I hired and then had to fire."

"How long did he work for you?"

"Just short of a year I think, just about a year. Fired him three years ago in June."

"Did you alone make the decision to fire Timmons or were the owners of the dairy involved?"

"Objection, leading," Petrakis loudly stated. He was fed up with Hirsh's bumbling around the courtroom.

"Overruled, answer the question," Danauet responded sneering at the plaintiff's table and rolling his eyes as the jury watched.

"Mr. Hirsh, I fired him all on my own. Never talked to the owners about it."

"Why did you fire Ray Timmons?"

"Because I was fed up with him. Poor attendance, tardy a lot, late on deliveries when he tried to pick up women on the route and came back to the warehouse smelling of mary jane a few times … Oh, and I forgot, we had customer complaints about him."

Petrakis rose to his feet with an objection to the hearsay testimony about unidentified customers making complaints. Danauet yawned, stretched and then overruled the objection despite its validity and importance.

"Mr. Tice, did you fire Timmons because he was black or complained of discrimination to you?"

"Absolutely not. I gave him a lot of rope and he hung himself with it." The not so subtle lynching reference hit Petrakis immediately and likely wafted over the heads of Hirsh and his paid for jurist.

"Judge, I pass the witness for cross-examination," Hirsh said.

Harry Petrakis was well known in Chicago for his trial skills and flawless preparation. No one prepared for trial better or with more enthusiasm.

Petrakis began: "Mr. Tice, you have methods for recording absences and tardiness of drivers at the dairy, don't you?"

"Well, my memory is pretty good about those things, so I rely on that quite a bit."

"For forty employees you rely on your memory?" Petrakis raised his voice and turned to the jury. "Aren't there some records that you keep of absences and tardiness?" Petrakis knew that Tice was lying under oath and toeing the company line at the trial. Mr. Tice was about to be dismembered as a witness.

"I don't keep any records of absences or tardiness. I know who I can count on and who I can't. Timmons flunked."

Petrakis went for the kill. "Mr. Tice, please take a look at Plaintiff's Exhibit 17. Do you recognize those records?"

Tice was handed a two-inch stack of lined documents with a chart on top. Names of drivers, warehousemen, dates and route assignments appeared on the sheets, two sheets for each day of the year Ray Timmons had worked for the company.

"Mr. Tice, those sheets in front of you are written out by you every day are they not?"

"Yes."

"And those sheets show who worked that day and what job and route the driver was assigned to that day, correct?"

"Yes, that is the system."

"Mr. Tice, do you see that summary chart on top of the daily route sheets? With the court's permission, Mr. Tice, that summary sheet identifies all the employees in all the underlying route sheets and tallies the days that the employees' names appear on a route sheet for the year that Ray Timmons worked at the dairy. It is undisputed that for a temporary driver like Timmons, perfect attendance in a calendar year would be 256 days. Now, what does the summary sheet say about the number of days that Ray Timmons worked that year?"

Reddening in the face in a bit to match his thinning red hair, Finnian Aloysius Tice meekly said, "254."

Petrakis underscored the number loudly while turning to scan the jury----"he worked 254 of 256 days and you fired him for absenteeism and being unreliable?" Three or four jurors snickered. Danauet glared at Hirsh and Khan.

Tice had no answer to that critical question, nor was he able to identify any specific customers who complained about Timmons' work or any specific days that he was tardy.

Tice was the dairy's key witness. He was stone cold dead on arrival.

"Judge, I am done with Mr. Tice and I pass the witness. Thank you Mr. Tice."

Micah Hirsh rose to lie again: "Judge, we see no need for redirect examination."

He then sat down, promptly giving way to his narcissistic notion that he was the peer of Gerry Spence, the famous trial lawyer from Jackson Hole, Wyoming.

The judge asked for the defense's next witness, to which Hirsh replied, "Carol Catherine Ryan, the president of Bowerman Dairy."

A six-foot-one-inch woman stuffed into a stunning navy blue with white piping Ann Taylor suit walked slowly to the witness stand. Her stout figure and thirty pounds of extra weight concentrated in the midriff now disguised the Division I athlete she had been in college. She had starred as a power forward on the University of Tennessee's dominating basketball team.

Carol Catherine Ryan, the granddaughter of the founder of the Bowerman Dairy Company, nestled into the comfortably grooved wooden witness chair looking pompous and immensely pleased with herself. A devout Catholic, she had been named after the petite and courageous Doctor of the Church, St. Catherine of Siena. Following Carol's birth, naming and baptism she and her namesake parted company once and for all.

Harry Petrakis was thrilled with the way Ryan looked. Everything that a wealthy business owner should not do in dressing for a jury trial in Chicago, Ryan had done. Neither she nor her inept lawyer knew any better. Petrakis and everybody else in the courtroom looked over at the four strands of large pearls she wore and the Rolex watch that was easy to spot.

Micah Hirsh got up to strut his stuff. "Mrs. Ryan, please tell the jury your name and your line of work."

"I am Carol Catherine Ryan and I run the Bowerman Dairy Company. The company has been in my family for three generations now since 1910."

Hirsh went on: "And, and … and … have you done any work for civil rights groups in the Chicago area?"

Petrakis leapt to his feet objecting to the irrelevance of this testimony and asking for a sidebar conference with the judge and Hirsh outside the hearing of the jury. Judge Danauet motioned the lawyers and the court reporter to join him in the hallway between the courtroom and the judge's library of detective fiction.

Danauet turned to Petrakis with a "What now, counsel?" Then, Danauet turned his attention to the court reporter's cleavage.

Petrakis paused a moment trying to overcome the stench of sweat from the judge. Then, he explained, "This is irrelevant because Mrs. Ryan had nothing to do with the decision to fire Timmons. Her civil rights work is irrelevant. She was not the decision-maker. This evidence is substantially outweighed by the prejudicial impact that it brings to the case. And, it is a waste of time. For both reasons it violates Illinois Supreme Court Rule 403 and should be excluded."

Danauet, still fixated on the reporter's freckled ample bosom, asked Hirsh for a response.

Hirsh merely said, "Judge, Mr. Petrakis won't like the witness' answer but the evidence shows that the company is racially tolerant. What better witness to prove that than the company president."

"The objection is overruled. Let's get this case to the jury." Danauet was privately grateful for the sexual fantasy break.

Everyone returned to the courtroom. Believing that he had a goldmine of a defense going, Hirsh moved his client into an explanation of her annual contributions to Catholic Charities, the wrongful execution defense projects of North-western University's Journalism School, the Southern Poverty Law Center and the American Civil Liberties Union. Petrakis made his continuing objection to all of this and was repeatedly overruled incorrectly.

Petrakis' cross-examination of Ryan was brief. She promptly admitted that she had not been involved in the firing of Timmons or in any conversations involving his campaign to become a union driver.

The defense then rested its case. After closing arguments the jury got the case, right after lunch on a Thursday afternoon at 1:30 p.m. In less than ninety minutes the jury returned a verdict in favor of Ray Timmons for $300,000—$150,000 in back pay and compensatory damages and $150,000 in punitive damages. Judge Danauet slurred a rote thanks to the jurors for their dedication to public service and sent them home early. He then entered the judgment on the verdict and then left the courtroom to the lawyers and their clients. Danauet returned to his chambers and placed a call to Carol

Lombard. She did not answer his call again.

Carol Ryan and Hirsh returned to his law office in a cab.

"Micah, you fucking asshole. You incompetent fucking asshole. Now, what are we going to do? You have no fucking idea how to practice law against a real lawyer like Petrakis. You can't even make a bribe work." She was screaming at her disheveled fixer all throughout the short cab ride to Hirsh's office.

Once in his office Hirsh reached for the bottle of Jack Daniels that he kept as a bookend for a twenty-five-year-old evidence treatise he had stolen from the Cook County law library. He downed a couple of shots and offered some to Ryan who declined.

"Get that fat fucker on the phone. I want to talk to him."

"Carol that is not a good idea. Let me handle this."

"You have been handling this and we just lost it all, you stupid shit. What are you going to do?"

Hirsh downed another shot. "Listen, I am going to call the judge now and put him on speaker. Just listen, do not talk. Let's figure out what went wrong."

Hirsh hit the speaker button on his phone and rang up Judge Danauet's direct line. The judge answered.

"Judge Danauet, this is Micah Hirsh. What's going on here?"

"What do you mean what's going on? I helped you in every way I could during the trial. I humiliated Petrakis before the jury whenever I could. I bounced qualified minority jurors off your jury. And I allowed in all that irrelevant evidence about your client's financial support for the niggers and the gays and the spics. You have no beef with me. I am not going to lose my gig with anything obvious enough to get the attention of the U.S. Attorney in Chicago. You fucked up. You had no defense to this case. You should have settled it a long time ago. Fuck you. You got your money's worth."

Carol Ryan got up, stormed out of the office and slammed the door in her wake.

"Judge, what is it going to take to overturn the verdict on a post-trial motion?" Hirsh asked.

"$25,000 in thirty days. You will have your ruling before Labor Day weekend."

"OK, that is more like it. I will talk to the client right away." The line went dead.

Carol Ryan approved the deal though she made sure that the money was deducted from Hirsh's fees for the jury trial work—which was as Danauet and Petrakis knew—incompetent. And, Evan Danauet shortly before Labor Day delivered a brief five-minute oral ruling with no proper legal basis overturning the jury verdict for lack of a scintilla of evidence of race discrimination. Harry Petrakis and his poor client were left with a winnable appeal to the Illinois Appellate Court in Chicago. For the time being Ray Timmons was out $300,000 and Petrakis' law firm had lost $150,000 in attorneys' fees and $7500 in costs advanced on a contingent fee case.

The economics of desperation took over. Timmons was desperate for money and could not find steady work. Petrakis' law partners were furious at him and their lost investment and the prospect of a year-long appeal followed by a retrial. In private settlement negotiations the Dairy agreed to pay Timmons $25,000 and Petrakis' firm $10,000 to end the litigation. The paltry payments amounted to a surrender by accepting seven percent of the real value of the case.

On September 15th Micah Hirsh and Harry Petrakis appeared in Judge Danauet's courtroom to advise him that a settlement had been reached requiring a stipulated dismissal of the case.

"Counsel, I am very happy to hear this. It was time to stop the fighting. I am glad you all came to your senses."

Petrakis could still smell the judge.

Some things never change, Petrakis mourned to himself as he walked out of the Daley Center. And it appeared that once again that the state court in Chicago was not quite ready for reform.

Fame;
Quindlen &
Hemingway*

Saturday, January 10, 2015, 11 a.m.
Uptown
North side of Chicago

CHARLES MARTINEZ, M.D., SLID INTO a comfortable chair in the bay window of The Magnolia Café

on Wilson and beckoned the waiter with the white-framed glasses. He ordered two Manhattans and drank both of them in under ten minutes as he waited for Peter to arrive. The bourbon warmed him all the way to his toes. His confidence for the debate surged. Charlie knew both American and world literature and writing technique far better than Peter did, though Peter would never admit it. *Hubris, that is what Peter suffered from. And,* Charlie thought, *he should know better, given his Greek heritage.*

Charlie arrived early for this important meeting, knowing that Peter, the other Director of the Old Irving Park Literary Society, would soon show up full of himself, strong opinions and a few facts about the writers up for election to the Society. Anna Quindlen's nomination had been tabled at the last directors meeting so Charlie could study her work. Peter had nominated Quindlen and had given a pretty convincing pitch for her election. The tabling of her vote for admission had led to violent riots in Lincoln Park, Hyde Park and the North Shore, which only quieted with the arrival of the Illinois National Guard. A number of bookstores had been ransacked in the frenzy.

Charlie enjoyed his buzz as he toyed with the idea of doing something unprecedented in the 239-year history of the Society—bringing up for reconsideration a candidate that had been voted down just one meeting ago. Charlie wanted Ernest Hemingway inducted into the Society and planned to raise hell about it if he had to. He braced himself for the debate with the loud-mouthed Greek and raised his arm beckoning the white-framed waiter again.

"Yes sir, what can I bring you? And, excuse me for asking, but are you walking or driving home?"

"I would like another, thank you very much and how I am getting home is none of your business." Charlie raised the empty glass, his hand trembling a bit. He had never had three Manhattans at 11:15 in the morning on an empty stomach before. The reaction was highly enjoyable. The drinks loosened him up, sparking a host of new arguments in favor of Hemingway's reconsideration. He wondered how much alcohol had contributed to the creative work of Sinclair Lewis, Hemingway and Tennessee Williams.

"Coming right up, but may I place your order for lunch?"

"Probably a good idea, given the serious boozing that is going on. Get me that order of short ribs with mac and cheese topped with onion rings. Bring two orders. My friend will be here any minute. He eats anything he wants thanks to his marathon running and tennis." Charlie scowled a bit.

"Happy to do that, sir." White frames sauntered off weaving his way expertly through the small restaurant of a dozen tables and an intimate polished bar with eight chairs. An eight-by-ten-foot framed print of Manet's *Olympia* graced the bar, the sight of which contributed mightily to the drinking that went on there. Charlie knew enough to keep Peter's back to the beauty or no business would ever get done that afternoon.

Peter pulled up in front of the bistro in his freshly washed yellow BMW convertible. He jumped out of the car, delicately negotiating his way through piles of snow from last week's eleven-inch storm. Upon reaching the sidewalk twenty feet west of the restaurant, he met a gaggle of reporters who jostled him, pressing for information about which writers might be voted into the world renowned Society today. Like any vain trial lawyer or average Illinois politico, Peter loved the attention. *Not quite like doing a jury trial in a "bet the bank case,"* he thought, *but quite a high.*

He was happy to recognize reporters from *The New York Times, Slate, The Huffington Post, Le Monde* and *The*

Washington Post and annoyed to see one from *the Chicago Tribune,* a paper he detested for its mediocrity and Republican slant on the news.

A Minneapolis journalist and disciple of Garrison Keillor spoke up: "Say, Peter, what can you tell us? Charlie gave us nothing to work with. Very boring out here, not to mention real goddamn cold—nothing to write about. No one wants to hear about the Society directors drinking themselves under the table. Dr. Martinez just ordered his third cocktail and it is only 11:30 a.m."

Katsaros smiled. "Charlie, my dear friend, must be getting himself in the mood to talk about Hemingway, the lounge lizard. I am sorry I cannot help you folks until after the votes are taken. We have traditions and decorum in the Society. I intend to honor them."

Peter moved through the group and pushed open the restaurant door with a notebook and a folder tucked under his arm. He enjoyed talking about writers with Charlie and being at the zenith of the literary world as a director of the Society. The meeting about to begin was the equivalent of Oscar night to the literary world. Admission to the Society had eclipsed the Nobel prize for Literature a generation ago.

"Charlie, good to see you," said Peter, sliding into his chair. "Hope you did your study of these writers. There is a lot to be done and a lot at stake." He glanced out the window at the throng of journalists. "Those reporters are desperate for some news. It is going to be hell getting out of here. I have asked the Mayor to give us a police escort home. He is thinking about it. We should allow some time for a press conference to announce the results."

Charlie smiled, oozing the wisdom and charm that only a human encyclopedia of literature and the humanities could muster.

"Hey, Peter, I ordered you your favorite dish. Should be here in about fifteen minutes. Order yourself a real drink. I am two ahead of you."

"So, I heard."

"Tell me how many miles run, tennis matches played and crunches done in the last week? I know the Olympian bragging is coming. Let's get on with it."

Peter laughed. Laughter came easy, happiness his preferred state of mind. In fact, it was a family tradition—a *Greek* family tradition he will remind you.

White Frames appeared and Peter ordered two Long Island Iced Teas but asked for them to be spaced about thirty minutes apart, so he could keep his wits about him.

Charlie boldly made the first move. "Peter, let's take another look at Hemingway. I think the Society will lose some of its prestige if we keep him out. I read quite a bit of his work. It was lean, mean, masculine and a big influence on the best writers that followed him. He won the Nobel Prize in Literature in 1954. That says a lot."

Peter had anticipated this approach and was ready with a rejoinder. "He was a narcissist who just about drank himself to death and treated some of his wives like chattel. Just finished reading a biography of Martha Gellhorn, Hemingway's third wife and a fine war correspondent and novelist. Her six-year relationship with Hemingway showed how mean, selfish and unstable the man was. All he wanted from Martha after a year-and-a-half courtship, while two-timing his second wife, was a drinking buddy and sexual partner on demand. It was all about Ernest worship."

"Now, I cannot disagree with you about the place he has in world literature, but his character is what bothers me so much."

Charlie, a former seminarian, finished off his third drink

and leaned forward to press his point. "Peter, if character were a criterion for this decision, then your favorite Society inductee, Sinclair Lewis, would never have been elected. I just finished an eight-hundred-page definitive biography of him by Mark Schorer. Lewis was the first American to win the Nobel Prize for Literature in 1920. And, believe me, he deserved it. But, he treated his wives just as badly as Hemingway, if not worse, while also drinking himself to death. You and I voted Lewis in at the last meeting, not giving a whit about his character."

Peter smiled in the face of defeat.

"Charlie, I cannot argue with you. Taking a cue from baseball's Hall of Fame, let's admit Hemingway today and keep Lewis in, of course, but add an asterisk next to their names for questionable character. Both our interests and points of view will be respected and the reputation of the Society assured."

"I am fine with that," Charlie promptly responded, laughing to himself how he had brought justice and equity to this nomination and bested his trial lawyer friend at his own debating game.

Literary history was made that afternoon when the first motion to reconsider a vote by the Old Irving Park Literary Society in 239 years was made and approved, as bad boy Ernest Hemingway was admitted to the Society.

Peter stepped out of the restaurant into the cold to face the reporters with news of the first vote of the day. "Hemingway is in. It was the Society's first motion to reconsider." The journalists murmured their approval as they tweeted the news world-wide. Within a few minutes they were reporting to Mr. Katsaros that the National Organization of Women had condemned this admission, while the National Rifle Association, Newt Gingrich, Rudy Giuliani and the Tea Party Caucus of the Republican party were wildly enthusiastic.

The biggest news following Hemingway's admission was a tweet announcing that the Koch brothers had made a gift of $110 million to the Literary Society in appreciation of the admission of their beloved Ernest.

White Frames appeared with two heaping plates of comfort food and Peter's first Long Island Iced Tea. The tea was gone in seconds and five minutes passed in silence for the savoring of the moist ribs and onion rings. Peter then decided that a beer would best follow over another Long Island, so White Frames was asked to substitute.

Peter then said, "Charlie, we have to make a final decision on Anna Quindlen. I have studied her work thoroughly and am wild about her. Her *Rise and Shine* novel about the virtues of sisterhood is such a fine book that I bought it for my wife and daughters.

"Quindlen has such a range in her writing—handling essay, opinion and novel writing with equal skill. Her *A Short Guide to a Happy Life* is a brilliant philosophical photo essay on love and virtue and balance, full of mantras of hope. I turn to it at least once a month for inspiration."

Charlie pondered this, then said: "I read both those books and a collection of her *New York Times* columns and found her as outstanding as you say. Unlike Lewis and Hemingway I think she should be admitted and she needs no asterisk—her character is about as fine as one could have."

"Well, I am very happy to hear that, Charlie. You worried me a bit when you asked to table the vote last meeting."

"I did need some time to think about it and go back and review her stuff. She is every bit as good as you say she is."

Both men sat back, finished off their mac and cheese and ribs. Peter drained his Stella feeling a deep satisfaction with the food, the votes and himself.

"Charlie, you handle the press with the admission of

Quindlen while I warm up the car to drive you home."

The bill was paid. White Frames was rewarded with a handsome tip. Peter waved goodbye to *Olympia* and pushed open the door of the bistro. Charlie stepped into the scrum of reporters.

"We are pleased to tell you that Anna Quindlen has been admitted to the Society for her fine contributions to literature and humanity."

The reporters all applauded and the praise went straight to Charlie's head.

"Now, if you will excuse me, Mr. Katsaros and I have to head home. Next week we will be meeting to talk about constructing the Society's first building with some of the funds that the Koch brothers just donated to our coffers. We have been very impressed with the stunning design of the The Poetry Foundation up on Superior in River North and would like to design and build an edifice just as impressive.

"Peter and I are not looking forward to the political fights that will break out over the location of the Society. Bridgeport and the 11th Ward Democratic Organization have already offered money and some patronage workers if we locate there. And, a relative of Blago has texted me that the former Governor has a 'fucking golden' idea for a spot. I know he wants something in return but there's no need to worry about him. He will be in the pen in Colorado until 2024 as it presently stands."

Charlie ambled through the snow drifts and into the warmed up yellow BMW for the short trip to their homes in Old Irving Park. The Mayor had sent a police escort. The directors were grateful.

Essays

Voltaire and Madame du Châtelet at their wedding
November 30, 2013

Aphrodite

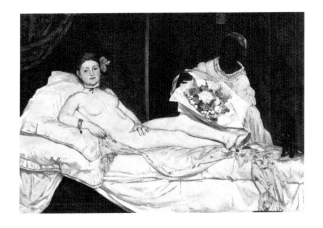

July 12, 2014

THREE MONTHS AGO I MARRIED a goddess—the one of love and beauty—the laughter loving one, the one who beat Hera and Athena in the Judgment of Paris. Thanks be to God for this union, and for the one before it that after twenty-six years of love and devotion sadly ended in an early death.

We were married by a true priest, a priest elected by the goddess and me, just like Voltaire did at Ferney. When you find a priest worth listening to, an admirable man—big hearted, loving and generous, like his saintly wife of many years—hire him. Millions pursue good priests and often settle for mediocrity. But, not me and Aphrodite. We do not tolerate mediocrity.

We were married on a sunny mild winter day on an Atlantic blue lake north of Chicago and north of Thanksgiving.

Aphrodite has a figure and a soul to die for. Klimt and Rodin would have immortalized her and tried to bed her. Her silver dollar breasts are a moveable feast. Thanks be to God.

The goddess stands taller than me in generosity and is ferocious in her defense of me, our four children, four grandchildren and family ways.

The flags of our fathers' homelands—Greece and Israel—sport the same hopeful sea blue hues. And our fathers—strong, indefatigable, loving, kind men—applaud from afar, along with their strong wives, whose hugs and encouragement strengthen us daily.

On the day Aphrodite and I wed, the smile on her face was the broadest and most natural I have seen. It has remained with her every day since. Her smiles beget my smiles and the sunshine, inside and outside my soul.

Marriage is sacramental in the faiths I know most about and for many good reasons.

If Paris stole my Aphrodite away to Troy, I would try and summon all the Greek chiefs to join me in a seafaring campaign like Menelaus did so long ago.

Problem is: the Greek chiefs are mainly broke, the Onassis trust probably owns the best ships—and that's that.

But, Paris will never squire Aphrodite away from this splendid union. Thanks be to God.

The Tough Guy

Son of a Tough Guy

Son of a Tough Guy

H E STOOD ABOUT FIVE-FIVE BUT just shy of six-ten in the shadow he left behind.

He was wiry and strong, having lived a long, arduous life starting in his boxing days, and later moving into twelve-hour, six- and seven-day workweeks with no vacations.

He was a man made of steel, extraordinary toughness, grit, hustle and drive.

He was courageous, coming to America as an orphan in 1920, hungry and longing to be with his three older brothers, who brought him to Chicago from Tripolis, Greece.

He was a diplomat, wise in the ways of the world. He chose his words carefully, listened carefully and taught his sons all he knew.

His two boys, tutored by his sunlit, cheerful example, learned quickly that extraordinary hustle and drive and ambition and having an education and running your own business in America can bring endless rewards, but that genuine happiness—the Greek family kind—can only be found in the frequent embrace and kisses of your wife and children.

I, the eldest son, think of this tough guy every day with the greatest fondness, love, admiration and gratitude—very much in admiration of his grit, but even more thankful for his warmth, cheerfulness and total devotion to his family. For his constant encouragement of me. For the hundreds of warm hugs and kisses. For the smiles that lit up his face whenever he saw me or talked to me or anyone in the big Greek family that we grew up in.

His work days started at five in the morning, as many of mine have. And, like him, I have worked six weeks in a row with one day off without complaint.

When I was the first in the college library in the morning and the last to leave, all I was doing was mirroring his work—though I was captivated by learning and still am.

And now, when I am often the first in the law firm to start work in the morning and often the last to leave, I cannot help but think of him as the door to the firm opens and closes with a click.

I have a joyful photo of him and my cherished Mother in my writing room at home and in my iPhone, so I will never be away from that great love of God.

For that is all God is—parental love like his and my Mother's—immensely beautiful, constant, generous love.

Love Letters

I AM BIG ON TRADITION AND fortunately was born into it. Learned the importance of traditions and fidelity from the Greeks who loved me so well and still do. Love the rootedness in life that traditions have given me and my loved ones—like love letters.

My dear mother, Anita, a lovely brunette with a great heart, ready smile and perfect penmanship, sent me weekly letters every week I was in college with news from home and encouragement and a $10 bill. The letters arrived on time each and every week in a small envelope—usually six or seven pages of sweetness and hope and kindness—all that my parents were about.

Now, that I think about it, my Father wrote his only sister, Thea Pitsa, back in Tripolis, Greece but less often than Mom wrote me. And so the letter writing tradition started as the love hit the page. Churchill wisely said, "Words are the only things that last forever." Perhaps, that is one reason my mother wrote me. It is certainly one of the reasons I wrote our three children every week they were away at college.

Our oldest child, Sarah, left for college in New York City in August 1997. My heart broke as Beth and I drove the eight hundred fifty miles to Greenwich Village and moved her into her twenty-story dormitory on the New York University campus. NYU was the perfect school for this brilliant, hard-working, artistic, internationally travelled urban sophisticate. Giving Barnard the back of her hand, Sarah loved NYU so much that she stayed for twelve years and sashayed out with one of their Ph.D. hoods at the tender age of twenty-eight. Just like her mother who got her graduate degree the same year Sarah was conceived, Sarah defended the doctoral dissertation while her three-month-old daughter, Molly, bided her time with her dad, Steve, outside the conference room.

I spent a good hour or more with each letter to Sarah trying to hide my grief, be humorous and encouraging and interesting. First thing Monday morning I dispatched my love letter for the earliest pickup by the mail carrier in my business building in Chicago's Loop. The letters kept us close and meant a lot to her and me. Sarah wrote about the lift the letters gave her in an essay she wrote for some writing class that I came upon recently in cleaning the family home. For me, my heart was revealed in my words.

I am pretty sure that, in closing all those letters, I repeated the words of my father, Michael, "We love you more than anything in the whole world." Love is our finest tradition.

One of the most heartwarming moments I can recall in recent years is when Sarah told me she kept every one of those letters. You just cannot beat love and tradition. And, I expect that Sarah and Steve will be writing Molly love letters whenever they are apart.

Kathryn Katsaros Lesher & Sarah Dennis

Kathryn A. Katsaros

Totally Unnecessary Drama

IT WAS DECEMBER OF 2004. I found myself deep in the bowels of Rush Hospital at 6:30 a.m. on a weekday watching my gorgeous daughter Kathryn pose for a photo shoot—1000 high-speed photos to be exact—of her aching back. Stunningly beautiful, this twenty-year-old aspiring classical ballet dancer was about to dance her heart out in leading roles in Nutcracker ballets in Chicago and on her second professional contract in Madison, Wisconsin. Thirteen ballet performances over the next two weeks. That was the goal, but pain and a possible stress fracture in her spine stood in the way.

The best orthopedic doc in the great metropolis of Chicago was hired to take the photos, read the photos and opine on the risks of dancing this marathon in the holiday season. Dancing on a stress fracture would risk a disabling injury that would keep Kathryn out of dance auditions for professional companies for six months or more.

I sat there listening to the high speed camera whirring, cracking jokes to keep Kathryn amused and hopeful and grateful for the ability to bring the best medicine had to offer to this fine young woman. This doctor, whose name has been lost to me, ministered to the best dancers and athletes in town. Getting him to care for Kathryn on short notice was again something for which I was deeply grateful and more than a bit amazed.

The whirring of the camera stopped. Ten or twenty minutes passed. Kathryn dozed on the exam table. I am sure I prayed a prayer or two.

All those prayers were answered. The famous doc walked in with the news that there was no fracture and Kathryn was free to dance those leading roles. We were elated, found our way out of Rush looking for some more coffee.

And, then as we wound our way out of this citadel of medical science, Kathryn mumbled these immortal words: "Dad, all of that, you know, was totally unnecessary."

I love Kathryn deeply and am grateful to her for many, many reasons. One of them is that she always cuts to the chase with words that are hilarious and unforgettable.

A Greek Guy's Lament

A LAMENT, THE OXFORD ENGLISH DICTIO-NARY says, is "a passionate expression of grief or sorrow." I think that fits what I am about to tell you.

Now, to get you in the Greek frame of mind for a lament, let us turn to the "old country." I don't know that much about the "old country," where my father and his family nearly starved to death in the early 20th century. But I know enough from the family stories (and the haunting film and book *Eleni*) to know that funerals in rural Greece in the early 20th century were often attended by a dozen professional mourners keening behind the coffin and the family. I can hear the wailing as I write.

My lament, though not musical, is dramatic. Some months ago, I had to sue a church school for a client, that was run by the same national church group that had much to do with launching me into a love affair with learning. The church group ran the high school that gave me an outstanding college prep education. And, after surviving my lament, I loved every second of the litigation.

Didn't Micah tell us to: "do justice, love kindness and walk humbly with God"? Sure he did. I followed this just command in filing the suit in the federal court in Chicago. These religious hypocrites deserved it. Elmer Gantries in clerical collars and holding the principalship of a grade school.

Sinclair Lewis, in the grand tradition of Voltaire, Twain and Mencken nailed religious hypocrites with his powerful 1925 novel, Elmer Gantry. I nailed them again in my own way with my 2011 lawsuit.

Why a lament then? Well…

I was a kid in the 8th grade attending an outstanding public school on the south side of Chicago, the eldest son of two thrifty entrepreneurial Greeks. My parents did what dozens of Chicago Greeks were known for: they loved their children above everything else and started their own businesses.

So, Michael and Anita Katsaros came to their eldest son—that would be me—and spoke with the directness for which Greeks were known. Their words went something like this. "Peter, we cannot afford to send you away to college, but we can afford to send you to the best private high school in the area. We will invest in you and if you do well, you may win a college scholarship. If that does not pan out, you can go to college in Chicago and live at home."

The die was cast. In September 1964 my parents delivered me, together with their deepest dreams and prayers, into the hands of the Lutheran Church Missouri Synod's high school, Luther South, sitting right on the southwestern tip of Chicago.

The school and the education I got was one of the greatest gifts I have ever been given. And those gifts are the wellspring of this lament. My high school experience was so joyous as to be almost mythical in the deep happiness I had in those four years.

My parent's investment, my love for learning and the dread of being coffined in the restaurant business was fertile soil for the superb secondary education that Luther South provided me. A dedicated faculty, most of them with Master's degrees, cutting-edge math and science curricula and rigorous training in research, essay writing and public speaking was the formula for success. Music and drama, student politics, journalism, wonderful loving friendships, state-of-the-art labs and athletic facilities graced us all.

My parents' investment worked. The Lutherans and their flagship school opened the doors for me to academic scholarships to Big Ten universities and elite private schools. My college education was exciting, absorbing and free.

What about the lament, the keening, the black garb of the grieving Greeks that I grew up hearing about and promised you at the start of this essay? Here we go:

In the spring of 2010 my law firm was visited by a petite fifty-eight-year-old woman who had dedicated her professional life, enormous industry and her heart to teaching in a Lutheran Church Missouri Synod grade school in a northwest suburb of Chicago. Married to a devout Lutheran man and often attending Lutheran services twice on the weekend, this woman at the zenith of her career had been staggered by a layoff, allegedly due to a fiscal crisis at the school and its parent church.

I probed into the facts in our first meeting. We talked for about two hours, reviewing her outstanding career and the facts surrounding the layoff. By the end of the two-hour interview the evidence revealed that this woman had improperly been selected for termination because she was married, an older worker and a woman. Her employer poorly masked the reasons for the layoff behind a fictional "budgetary" problem. I opined that she had been the victim of employment discrimination. I recommended that she file suit under federal and state law to regain both her job and the hundreds of thousands of dollars of damages that were accruing due to the premature end of her career. My client liked what she heard and authorized me to approach the school to try and settle the matter in lieu of litigation. I did that. I was told figuratively to go to hell. I had a better idea. I filed the suit.

My lament, quite honestly, lasted a tenth of a nanosecond. There was no keening. I never donned black. I think I wore a navy Brooks Brothers suit and tie the day we filed suit.

I have always hated religious hypocrisy since I first encountered it in childhood in the Greek Orthodox Church. This lawsuit was just another scandalous exposure of hypocrisy by the clerics.

These Elmer Gantries picked on the wrong woman and educated the wrong kid.

A Chicago Greek in Exile; Wilmette, Ill.

IT IS NOT A PRISON. Actually, the neighborhood scenes are beautiful—Norman Rockwellian and straight out of *Yankee* travel magazine—most of them.

There are many more Republican George Babbitts at the oak-paneled Wilmette train station building than I am used to in the gritty open air Irving Park train stop near my former Chicago home. You see them—they clear their throats a lot, rarely smile (even when traveling with their wives or mistresses), they wear L.L. Bean winter boots or Totes for shoes (when there is only a ten percent chance of rain), they speak in deep, sonorous voices, and their couplings are no doubt brief and lackluster—so their wives can get to sleep and quickly forget the ordeals. Looking grim and wondering what their net worth will be when the market closes, chatting it up about golf and sailing and their children's trips abroad to study in worthless university programs in overpriced colleges.

No wonder Sinclair Lewis—America's first Nobel

Laureate in Literature in 1930—drank himself to death. He was trapped and strangled—surely by alcohol and paralyzing, untreated mood swings—but equally so by the George Babbitts that ran America in the 1920's. Hell, they still do, ever since the Democrats stopped acting like Democrats when Jimmy Carter became President in 1976.

Dear Lord, I thought most lawyers were boring until I moved to Wilmette, IL in pursuit of my great wife (who is quite lovely thank you very much).

Two years ago I moved from Chicago—one of the world's great cities—a place that nurtured me and my Greek families, educated me well, taught me street wisdom—a very gritty Democratic town known for its brilliant Mike Royko (another wonderful satirist and drunk like Lewis), generations of corrupt pay-to-play politicians, racial divides, usually small-minded Catholic archbishops, and a U.S. Attorneys' office working 24/7 on public corruption cases. Nelson Algren's take on the city still rings true. "Living in Chicago is like being married to a woman with a broken nose. There may be lovelier lovelies, but never a love so real."

Now, I have been exiled to some painful, mind-blowing, exhausting, sleep-inducing conversations with some incredibly self-absorbed North Shore folks.

That old adage about the University of Chicago ("where fun goes to die") is horribly misplaced. Fun and good conversation dies thousands of times daily on Chicago's North Shore.

Upper middle class North Shore types complain about minutiae (*ice on the sidewalks! What a concept in the upper Midwest!*)—traffic on the expressways (*weren't the expressways built just to usher the North Shoreans 21 miles to Chicago's Loop with no stops or slowdowns—shouldn't traffic only be for the working and the middle class?* they must be thinking). And how could I forget the foodies—dining out at overpriced restaurants, where the waitstaff is the best you could ever find but never good enough. These cookie-cutter personality types have lost sight of the hardship many Americans suffer daily, being so wrapped up in their self-absorbed worlds—especially the men—they are so very, very important and impressed with themselves.

Some North Shore men I have met should really consider going mute when they go out socially, so good conversation and genuine communication can proceed in spite of them.

I find the North Shore types who have found no time for learning or art or some creative self-expression incredibly tedious and worthy of a public shaming ritual or two. Thankfully for them, the U.S. Constitution stands in the way of that. What rot!

I take that back. I am a big fan of our Constitution.

When I took up this voluntary exile to the North Shore, I was madly in love—still am—hope she wakes up soon, I have a plan—

But, the dues I have had to pay in this romantic quest were hefty—many dead-end conversations in the intellectual wasteland of Chicago's North Shore. My wife is worth it.

The Humanities Newsletter

Editor and Publisher: Voltaire

Vol I, Issue 1

WELCOME TO THE FIRST ISSUE of this newsletter. It was conceived on Easter weekend 2014 on a glorious sunlit day in Chicago with temps in the low forties. The newsletter reflects Voltaire's current thinking and studying in the humanities and is given to encourage all of you to try out some of these books and plays and artistic pursuits. The newsletter will be published irregularly but always with enthusiasm and zest, because that is my mantra.

I went to the theatre weeks ago with the elegant Madame du Chatalet to see an outstanding play—*Tristan and Iseult*. The play was produced by The Kneehigh Theatre Company of Cornwall, England in co-operation with The Chicago Shakespeare Company. The actors were British and superb—each and every one of them. From the very first interactions of the audience and the actors, which occurred with some playful banter between the cast and the audience before the show began, the play was a delightful romp.

Within minutes of the start of the show I understood why people go into acting and the theatre. When the acting works and the actors and playwright connect with the audience, nothing in the world is more fun. This play's modern take on the several medieval versions of this tale sported a five piece band, fine female vocalists, dance and gymnastics, fight scenes and of course, love and pathos.

Kneehigh is on a tour through the U.S., that jump started at The Berkeley Repertory Theatre in Berkeley, California. Kneehigh is a superb group of actors and directors who give all their audiences a highly sought after gift: captivating entertainment. Hats off to The Berkeley Rep, Kneehigh and Chicago Shakespeare for this show.

Another fine play that I recommend with a caveat is *Our Class*, a play by Polish playwright Tad Slobodzianek, now at Remy Bumppo Theatre in Chicago. This play shows all the horrors of the Holocaust, frightens the audience into praying that this never happens again, and then in an unfortunate turn of events goes on about half an hour too long, leaving most in the audience frustrated and furious at the playwright for doing so much to ruin a good thing.

Turning now to the book reviews in this debut issue, I highly recommend for all Chicagoans—wherever life has taken you—*The Third Coast,* a history of our windbag city with all its dimples and warts from 1930 to 1960. The book is a historical treasure trove of Chicago art and architecture, politics, music, poetry and fiction written in a flowing, frank and insightful style. We do have a magnificent *coast* in Chicago, that glorious 18-mile lakefront that thrills me every time I see it. This book is a delicious, well-researched and well-written read with zero calories, recently released in paperback.

Finally, for the poets, philosophers and athletes among us I have found a must read: *The Essential Sheehan* (Rodale Press

2013). Dr. George Sheehan was a New Jersey cardiologist, master's runner and essayist of the first rank. Upon discovering running in middle age, 45, and dropping his smoking and overeating habits, he launched into a period of self-discovery and joy which he generously shared with others in his essays on running, balance, fitness and faith.

Sheehan was a monthly columnist and running prophet for *Runner's World*, the leading running magazine in the U.S. Sheehan's 145 columns, public speaking and eight books helped launch the running boom in the States that started in the 1970s. This elegant book was developed by a couple of Sheehan's dozen children. Every essay is a gem. Whether you want to reflect on the joy of play, health, distance running, balance or the spiritual life, this book will get you there. I am buying this book for my family because they will all be wiser if they can get past my having recommended it and actually read it.

All the best,

Voltaire

Poems

How I Met the Poets in My Life

I REMEMBER IT CLEARLY. IT WAS a Friday night and I was in the family room of my cozy Chicago home in the warm embrace of family life. It was 1995. I was 45 years old.

Witnessing the poets plying their trade allowed me to enter another literary trance (love trances so much). I was captivated by the siren songs of this art form and the writers that peopled it. They were alive, brimming with zest for their work.

The show itself was a PBS series called *The Language of Life* featuring perhaps my dearest Muse Bill Moyers. He was interviewing poets at the Dodge Poetry Festival in Waterloo, New Jersey. I listened to about a half dozen poets as they proudly read their work with inspiring enthusiasm. They were joyful. I was hooked on their idealism and dreamy stories, the gleam in their eyes, the energy they radiated and the beauty of the language they sculpted. In my mind's eye, I saw images that were vivid and brilliantly colored, allowing me much clearer glimpses of the pleasures and losses of life than I had heard from any other writers before. These poets got to the point and - to my great pleasure - looked at life as I did: in a sensual way.

Fortunately for me, Mr. Moyers then published a book, also called *The Language of Life,* in which he synopsized the interviews and some poems from two dozen of the writers at the festival. That book became my mid-life primer on poetry. Every Saturday after my eight mile run, I would study the biography of the writer and then slowly read and reread their leading poems. I was thrilled to be introduced to (and then go on to read even more poetry from) Coleman Barks, Robert Bly, Lucille Clifton, Rita Dove, Carolyn Forché, Donald Hall, Robert Hass, Sharon Olds, Jane Kenyon, Stanley Kunitz, Naomi Shihab Nye, Adrienne Rich and Galway Kinnell. I have been hooked on poetry ever since. Many thanks to you, Mr. Moyers, for re-opening the door to this art form to me through your incredible program.

Shortly afterwards, I was introduced to the poetry of Mary Oliver, through the Catholic theologian and gifted story-teller/writer Jack Shea. For years Jack Shea has been spreading faith and hope generously in his Advent reflections at Old St. Patrick's Church in downtown Chicago. Mary Oliver was often the poet to whom he turned to make his points clear and remembered. I now have four volumes of her poetry under my belt and am grateful for everyone. I often read some of her poems to my wife, Joanne, as we journey through life together. So, I am thankful for Shea's mentoring and preaching and Ms. Oliver's word pictures.

Once I started seeking out good poetry, it seemed to be everywhere. I soon stumbled across Garrison Keillor's first two collections of poetry, *Good Poems* and *Good Poems for Hard Times,* as well as his soul enriching daily dose of poetry and the humanities in *The Writer's Almanac,* Keillor's online newsletter. Mr. Keillor selects the poems in each volume and then introduces them in a Twain-like essay brimming with wisdom and humor. Keillor writes frankly about some of his favorite poets and comments on their various styles, but he also highlights the importance of poetry as a source of hope for our society and humanity. The essays are brilliant for their scholarship, humor and love of truth and virtues. I return to them often for their refreshing and hopeful wisdom. I also strive to come close to their quality when I sit down to write.

Finally, if you have any faith or spiritual life (or thirst for one), go and read the poems Keillor collected for the "*God*" chapter of *Good Poems.* Trust me, you will return to them again and again during your spiritual and meditative times. *Karma, Dharma* is my personal favorite, so much so that I read it during my wedding last year and again at the weddings of both my daughters. Humor and faith and wisdom in ten lines or less—what a gift.

Mr. Keillor, through *The Writer's Almanac,* led me to the American poet, Charles Bukowski. I now have four of his collections and admire Bukowski's ability to paint absorbing pictures of working class city life in LA with clear, bold strokes and humor.

Closest to my heart, though—and my children know this well—are my earliest mentors in poetry: the Greeks. "The Greeks thought of everything," was the refrain that I used at dinner when our children were growing up. And certainly the Greeks' long epic poems have dominated literary mythology for centuries and will always be honored in the annals of world poetry.

I have in my memory bank thousands of golden moments from my life, but one of the happiest is my time spent reading a favorite book of Greek myths by the evening light of my parent's kitchen on South Winchester in Chicago.

I was eight or nine years old. My book of myths was about a hundred pages and included most of the episodes of *The Odyssey.* I remember being thrilled by the blinding of the Cyclops, the ingenuity of the Trojan Horse and Odysseus shooting the arrow through a dozen axe heads lined up before him. It was then, for the first time, that a book brought me, willingly, into a wonderful imaginative trance, not releasing me until the last page had been devoured. In time, that book literally fell apart from overuse and had to be reassembled every two weeks or so in order for me to return to ancient Greece. So my deepest thanks is given to Homer and Ovid and Edith Hamilton and all those wonderful classics scholars in Britain and America for their translations and scholarship on these timeless, epics.

Moyers, Shea, Keillor and Homer, I offer you my deepest gratitude for your splendid, generous gifts and imaginative teaching and writing. My life is happier, serene and wiser due to your work.

A Night to be Remembered

An exotic, candlelit bubble bath of deep kisses, soft talk, soothing voices, listening, warmth—angelic comfort—touching so dream-like

Rexrothian surely and surely Olympian—"The Greeks thought of everything," my children were told

We met soon after, her nipples moist and glistening in the candlelight

I thought to myself—she is Greek goddess like—why shouldn't she freshen them up like Aphrodite and her clan—loved it—loved them

Heaven followed, always so when imaginations are unleashed seeking and giving joy

Fantasies made real—thrilling times followed—deep, deep happiness—sacred serenity and peace

Marriage, love and fidelity are sacraments in my faith, cherished in hers

And, then another Olympian thrill falling asleep next to her bare melon breasts—nipples firm and alluring in the soft light—no beauty ever lovelier

Scores of romantic dreams coming true, then giving birth to hundreds more—my wife encouraging more dreams like these to be born

Thank God—my spectacularly sexy wife gets it!

God at the Window

I share a birthday with William Blake—that wonderful British poet and visual artist and evangelist of the imagination

Blake saw God and spiritual visions often and certainly saw the Divine as a shadow near one of the windows in his house in the engravers' neighborhood of London. I see Blake's window panes each morning during my morning prayers in the Green Room in this god-filled house that we live in

I carry some of Blake's finest poems with me every day in the briefcase of literary stuff that I dive into journeying to and from the law firm

Blake wrote what all the wisest spiritual teachers have said and what good psychologists tell you. The way to a happy life is to "Create a System or be enslav'd by another Man's." We are not to "reason & Compare: our business is to Create."

Obscure, you say

Not my poetry, never my poetry. You will get the message if you keep reading.

Joseph Campbell, another great spiritual scholar and religious anti-cleric (the only clerics I can stand—me and my buddies Voltaire and Emerson agree on this one) said it a different way

Campbell said that every person comes to a crossroads in his life at which time the decision must be made. Is the machine that is threatening to control you going to do that; or are you going to control the machine? If the machine controls, your soul is lost. If you control the machine, the good life is assured.

I am an American who daily encounters an American culture obsessed with secular virtues of wealth, celebrity, power and domination. That American machine daily tries to define me. I have never let it do so, though the struggle to fight that definition is not always easy.

In winning the struggle with the American machine I am reminded and encouraged by one of my Mother's greatest teachings. When I returned from grade school a bit dejected from not being able to run fast, she in her clear, confident voice showed me the way to beat the machine in saying: "We didn't send you to school to run fast. We sent you there to study hard and get an education." I never worried about running fast again.

Blake, Campbell and all the best spiritual writers underscored for me over the years my Mother's bold, clear message: define the good life for yourself. I heard them and am grateful to all of them for their courage, wisdom and generosity.

The Watering Can

It is two-thirty in the morning in my warm bed next to Aphrodite

I am thirsty and lustful

And dying to bring my watering can to her mountains and forest

Aphrodite—the inadvertent seducer

Reaching back into our voluminous love library, I recall with pleasure her sipping her early morning pre-run coffee, perhaps inviting me to breakfast in the bush

Never one to overlook a romantic clue, and

With the zest of a collegian and remembering my father's words about making love not war, I ate heartily reveling in the feast set for me in her cavern

My Aphrodite—wife and goddess of love and loving ways

Pink

This Victoria's Secret design fit snugly to her curvaceous figure as her breasts rose to greet me—a morning feast of zestful beauty that I had dreamed of

Her kisses were rich, deep—full of energy and enthusiasm for the ecstasy ahead

No one was disappointed

There is no greater love than this—now or since.

On Women and Fashion

I must do it

I really must do it after whining about it and being incensed about it for so, so many years

Hard to do, not really

Fun to do, certainly

Am I an authority?

Hell yes

My qualifications to opine on women's fashion, nothing short of a Ph.D., mind you

Married two gorgeous women who dressed well, the first one died young barely forty-nine—the second one, Madame du Châtelet , thriving at sixty-four with thirty years to go and with Olympian energy and style

What else?

Tutored in fashion by my Mother—a Greek beauty radiating a cheerfulness that I carry daily—she dressed smartly and with pizzazz on her modest budget

Mom and I shopped on Saturdays—window-shopped mainly in the department stores at 79th and Halsted on Chicago's south side

Where we lunched after shopping and laughed and laughed and laughed together—such ecstatically happy days

The bus rides down 79th street cost seven cents

Life was safe then—there was no cruelty in it that I had seen—that would change but not till my twenties

And after lunch we would buy transfers and hop off the bus at Loomis

And pop into the Chicago Public Library branch, where I wandered and pondered and dreamed big dreams

and hugged ten books—the legal limit—to take home and
get lost in

Still doing that

Mom taught me about color and fashion and beauty
and love

And the thousands of beautiful women I have seen
world-wide schooled me in beauty

And finally, I been to Paris on the recent honeymoon
with the hot wife, nestled in the honeymoon hotel—Hotel
Brighton—across from the Tuilleries Gardens

Surrounded by dozens of women's clothing stores
showing dresses in the loveliest of pastels and two toned
heeled shoes in dozens of interesting matches

There we window shopped and admired the height
of women's fashion and stopped for our café au lait in the
morning and afternoon—watching those fine Parisians
watching each other

I am qualified—that's the end of that—the *Daubert*
standard has been met

Let's start with women's shoes

The ones that drove me dizzy and crazy were the really,
really pointy heeled dress shoes—every time I saw a pair I
got scared remembering the pointy nose of the *Wicked Witch
of the East in the Wizard of Oz*

That witch had an ugly visage, that the shoe designers

immortalized in millions of pairs of shoes

That were foisted on young women and aggravated men like me—with such tender sensibilities—for years

The suffering I endured was immense and so undeserved

One of my daughters with the movie star looks defended the witch like shoes saying quietly

"They are really comfortable."

An unacceptable price for ugliness and cruelty to sensitive types like me, I reply

And then—women's scarves horrify me—driving me to the therapist's couch

Not a bad thing you say—the hot wife is a sexy therapist—not what I meant exactly

Admit it—a woman's beauty can be found in their countenance (a big Shakespearean word for face) and her figure and her soul. Soul is not my concern here—only fashion, stupid fashions

Here we have thousands of gorgeous women parading around Paris and Chicago and other classy cities hiding their beautiful figures behind *SCARVES*

In fawning subservience to the fashion gods—whoever the hell they are—

There were none on Olympus—for obvious

reasons—you have never seen a Greek goddess with a scarf covering her figure

The Greeks were far too smart for that

If women want to hide their lovely figures behind *SCARVES*, why not burlap bags or overcoats—why go half way?

I did it

I said my piece

And next time, I won't be shy about returning to critique fashion trends that my Mother and I would have dissed emphatically

Prayer

Happiness & Gratitude

Eight hours of sleep in the warmth of my erotic wife, interrupted only by memories of our thrilling, artistic embraces, our loving ways with each other, the constancy and hope that comes with feeling and celebrating our devotion to each other,

The soft, comforting sound of my wife's voice during a 5 am run down Poplar or Elmwood or Greenleaf Streets in Wilmette or in the evening in the living room or later in the evening in the quiet of the family room as we listen to each other, then encourage each other to hope and dream and act and never get discouraged by the harshness of the world,

Which will always be there, the Buddhists say so correctly but not despairingly

Morning prayer—praying for the Red Sea to part one

more time, today and every day, speaking the new and old prayers that have been answered for 40 years or more now, prayers that inspire my mornings and days, gazing on God at my window panes and at William Blake's window panes on the south wall in our Green Room at 4:15 in the morning,

Sitting here Sunday morning in a sunlit home putting sculpted words and memories on the page, warming my heart again and again, bringing the buoyancy and the sunshine of my soul out and encouraging the boy in me to go out and play some more and play hard, and laugh throughout the day, living life with abundance and gratitude and awe,

Loving the serenity of weekend mornings of solitude, a five-mile run by our blessed Lake Michigan—a captivating jewel—and through one fine neighborhood after another, forging new running paths down the enchanting Green Bay Road, watching the few people I meet wake up and find their ritual solitude,

Visiting my favorite orthopedic docs to be told that my 31-year divine running gift would keep on giving and more recently that my sore shoulder did not mean the end of my thrilling journey into tennis. Few people I know have docs and a physical therapist like these that only give "good news,"

Living a life full of four fine children and their loved ones—two recent weddings that were love fests, where I could speak from my heart about why my family life—all four generations of it known to me—is my greatest joy, a year now closing full of happy holiday parties and race celebrations and backyard parties and so many beautiful moments together, for which I should show more gratitude, wonder and awe,

So many genuine friends, that keeping up with them could be a glorious full-time job,

Thanks be to God for every one of them and you all know who you are,

Practicing trial work with zest, empathy, hustle, hope, imagination and enthusiasm, keeping hope and self-esteem alive in the suffering clients and being offended often by injustice—praying for more justice in a system burdened by mediocrity, narcissism, indifference and greed,

Such is my bounty of happiness, my spiritual lens on life and heaven, my heart, the light in the darkness that is always there,

The prophet Jeremiah was strong and resolute and right despite his difficult work,

God does have plans to prosper and not harm us, to give us hope and a future.

CPSIA information can be obtained
at www.ICGtesting.com
Printed in the USA
LVOW01s2031260516
489806LV00012B/35/P